This book belongs to:

_____

_____

Thank you for choosing *Fairy Homes in my Garden*

Coloring pictures is an enjoyable and accessible activity that offers a range of benefits for individuals of all ages and skill levels. This practice can help you find balance and tranquility in your daily life, whether you need stress relief, a creative outlet, or a moment of mindfulness. Witnessing the transformation of a blank page into a vibrant work of art can boost your self-confidence and self-esteem. It provides a tangible result that you can be proud of, regardless of your artistic background.

There is no right or wrong way to color illustrations. Use your imagination. Try a variety of tools—colored pencils, markers, pens, pastels, and crayons. If you use markers or pens, place a piece of cardboard or heavy paper so your coloring does not bleed onto the next page. The pictures appear only on one side of the paper to help with bleeding. It also allows you to remove a page for framing, if you wish. There is a page where you can experiment with mixing colors.

The fact that you have chosen to support my work warms my heart. I hope the book brings you as many hours of joy as designing it did for me. Know that these pictures were a labor of love. I am thrilled to know they have found a wonderful home with you.

Grab a cup of coffee or tea, sit down, relax, and have fun.
 You deserve some quiet time.

Thank you again for your support

Color Sampler

Not sure what color to use? Try it here or try mixing colors together

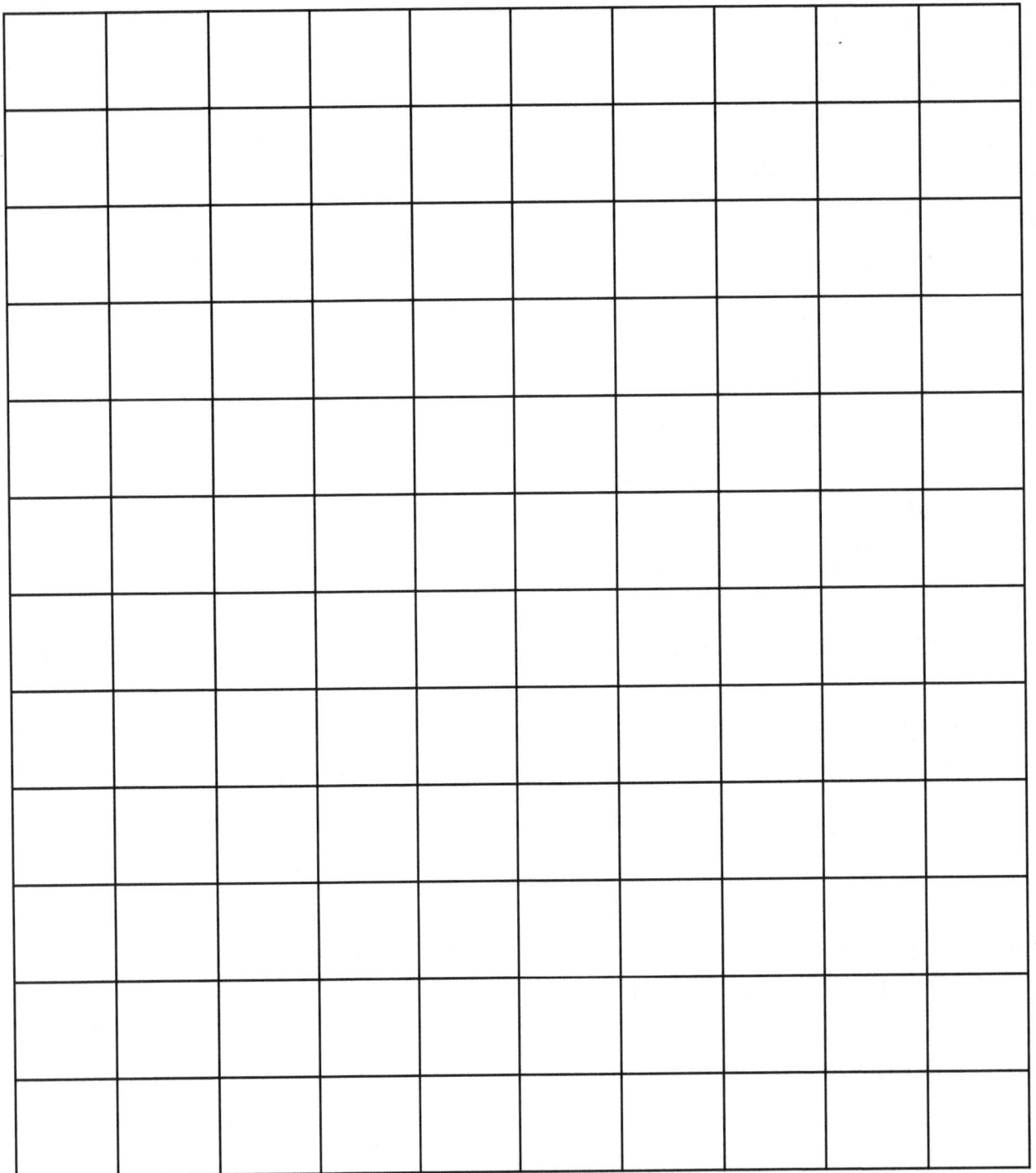

Congratulations. You've finished coloring all those beautiful Fairy Homes. I hope you had fun. If you enjoyed the experience, please leave me a review on Amazon.

To view more of my coloring books, please visit www.prgarcia1.com. Or check out my author profile on Amazon. Sign up for my newsletter and receive free coloring pages, coloring tips, and notification of upcoming releases.

Never forget to have a little fun every day. Spred goodwill throughout your world. And keep your eye out for one of those fairy houses. You never know when you might stumble across one.

Other adult coloring books available on Amazon

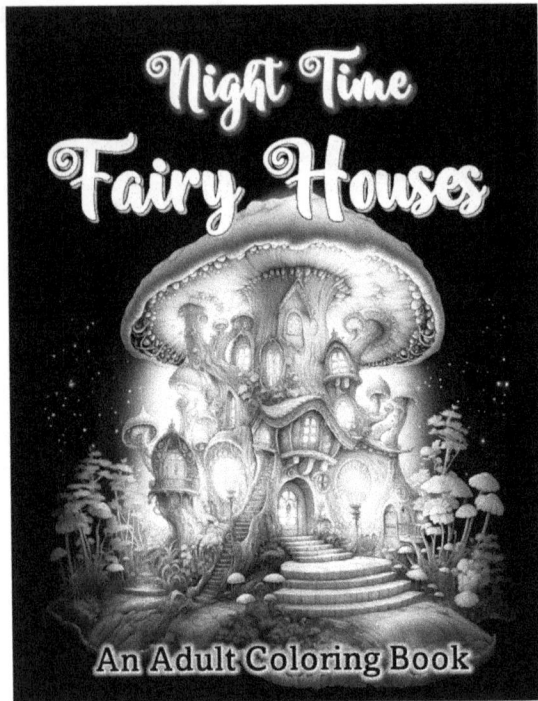

Night Time Fairy Houses
An Adult Coloring Book

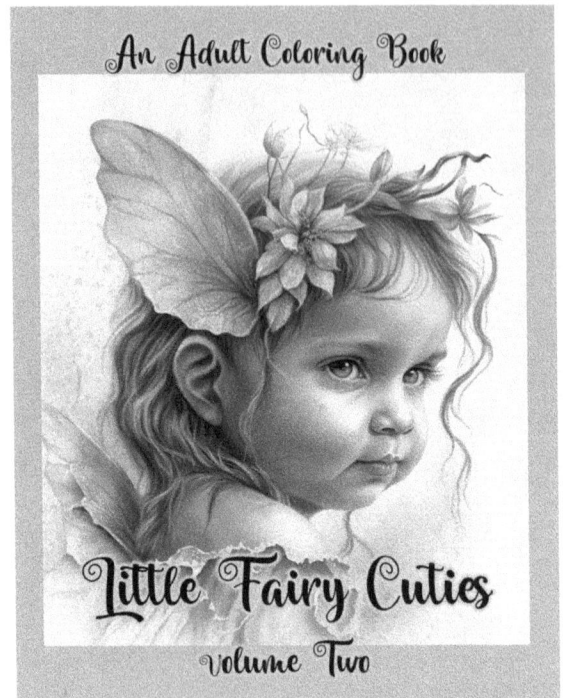

An Adult Coloring Book
Little Fairy Cuties
Volume Two

Enchanting Fairy Houses
An Adult Coloring Book

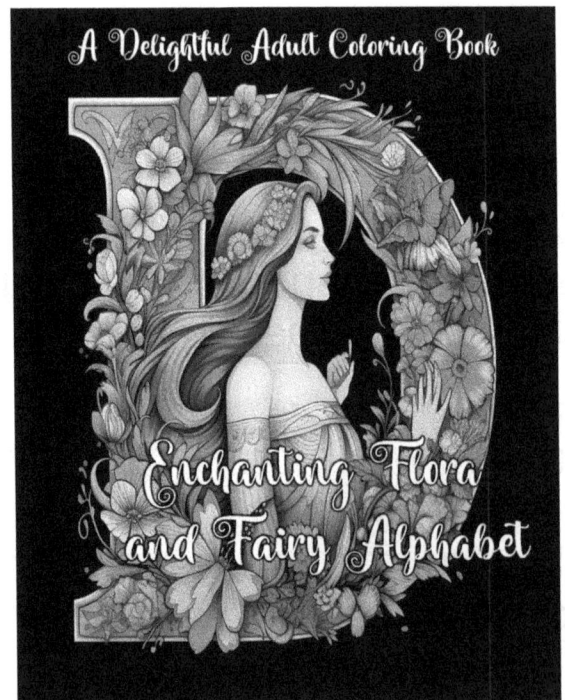

A Delightful Adult Coloring Book
Enchanting Flora and Fairy Alphabet

PRGARCIA1